FINISHING LINE PRESS
www.finishinglinepress.com

Sphinxlike

Chime Lama

Finishing Line Press
Georgetown, Kentucky

Sphinxlike

Would the owner of the golden 1963 Peel P50 please move their car.
It is blocking the fire hydrant.

ISBN 979-8-88838-397-1 First Edition

ACKNOWLEDGMENTS

Gratefully,
"686" appeared in *SWAMP Magazine*, Issue 24, 2019
"A Weaving" appeared in *Tiding House,* Issue 2, Summer 2022
"All My Pursuits" appeared in *Cadernos De Literatura*, Issue 24, 2021
"Become a Ball" appeared in *The Penguin Book of Modern Tibetan Essays,* 2023
"blue bird" (open and closed) appeared in *Volume Poetry*, Issue 5, 2021
"Buddha Hands" appeared in *SWAMP Magazine*, Issue 24, 2019
"Complete Phase Cancellation" appeared in *Inverted Syntax*, Print Issue 4, November 2022
"Grateful Criss Cross" appeared in *Pangyrus,* April 2022
"Ode to Sumō" appeared in *A Gathering of the Tribes Magazine Online*, 2021
"One City Day" appeared in *Volume Poetry*, Issue 5, 2021
"Peeking Om" appeared in *Stonecoast Review,* Issue 13, Summer 2020
"Soaring Bodies" appeared in *Stonecoast Review,* Issue 13, Summer 2020
"Table of Contents" and "Table of Contents II" appeared in *Cadernos De Literatura*, Issue 24, 2021
"Tibetan-American Anxieties" appeared in *The Margins*, 2019
"Trifecta" appeared in *Stonecoast Review,* Issue 13, Summer 2020
"Two Catches" appeared in *Street Cake*, Issue 69, Part 2, 2020

Publisher: Leah Huete de Maines
Editor: Christen Kincaid
Cover Art: Chime Lama
Author Photo: Todd Fleming
Cover Design: Chime Lama

Order online: www.finishinglinepress.com
also available on amazon.com

Author inquiries and mail orders:
Finishing Line Press
PO Box 1626
Georgetown, Kentucky 40324
USA

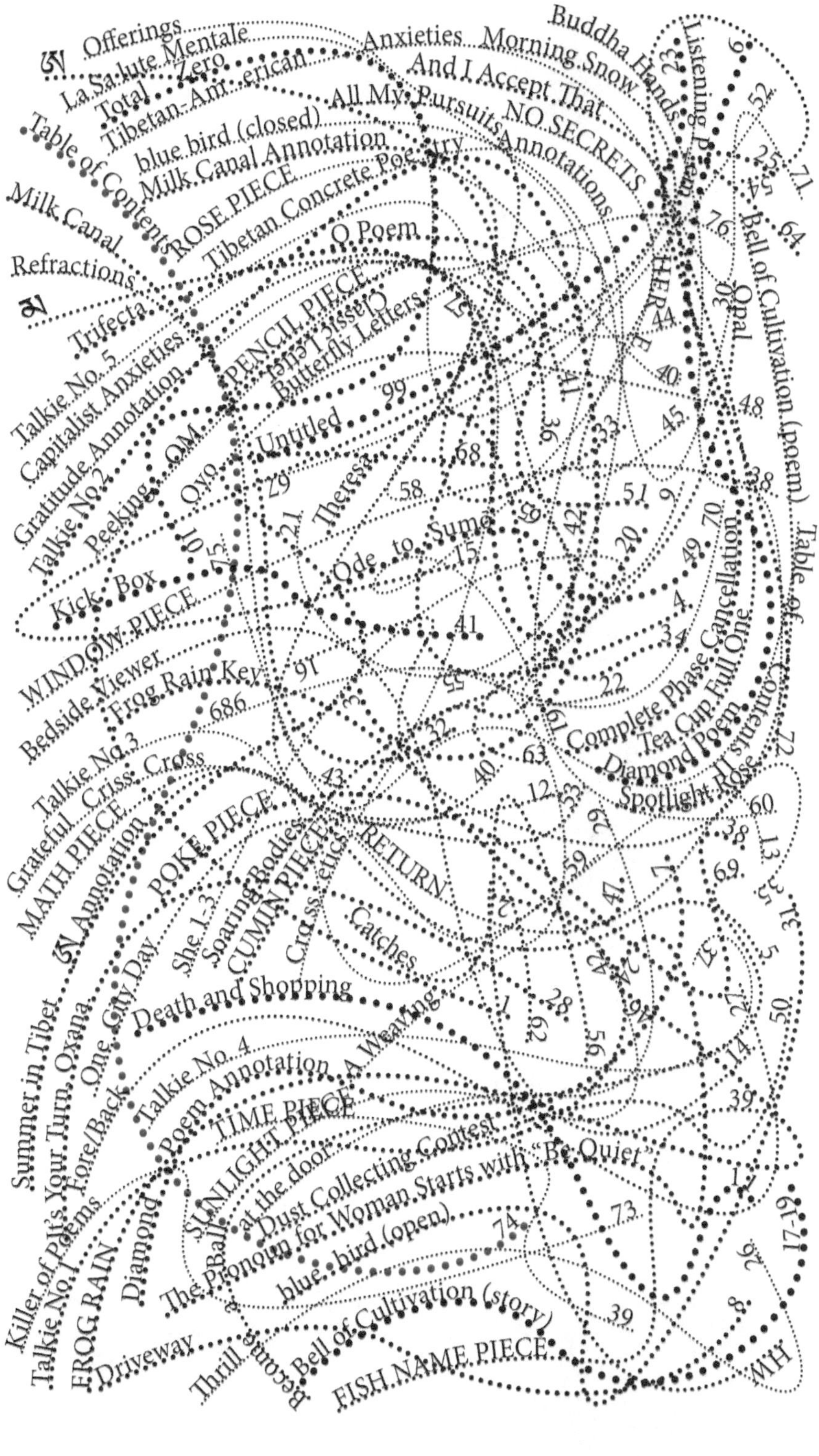
Offerings
La Salute Mentale
Total Zero
Tibetan-American
Table of Contents
blue bird (closed)
Milk Canal Annotation
Milk Canal
ROSE PIECE
Refractions
Tibetan Concrete Poetry
Trifecta
O Poem
Talkie No. 5
PENCIL PIECE
Capitalist Anxieties
Classic Letters
Butterfly Letters
Gratitude Annotation
Untitled
Talkie No. 2
OM
Peeking
Oyo
Theresa
Ode to Sume
Kick Box
WINDOW PIECE
Bedside Viewer
Frog Rain Key
Talkie No. 3
Grateful Criss Cross
MATH PIECE
Annotation
POKE PIECE
Soaring Bodies
CUMIN PIECE
RETURN
Cross-etics
Catches
She 1-3
Death and Shopping
Summer in Tibet
One City Day
Oxana
It's Your Turn
Fore/Back
Talkie No. 4
Poem Annotation
A Weaving
TIME PIECE
SUNLIGHT PIECE
Ball at the door
Dust Collecting Contest
The Pronoun for Woman Starts with "Be Quiet"
blue bird (open)
Killer of Pilt
Poems
Talkie No. 1
FROG RAIN
Diamond
Driveway
Thrill
Become
Bell of Cultivation (story)
FISH NAME PIECE
HM
Anxieties
Morning Snow
Buddha Hands
And I Accept That
All My Pursuits
NO SECRETS
Annotations
Listening
Bell of Cultivation (poem)
Opal
HERE
Table of Contents II
Complete Phase Cancellation
Tea Cup Full One
Diamond Poem
Spotlight Rose
17-19

Talkie No.1

Tibet. Tibet, I'll say it again. That place where the sun meets the moon. Tibet with cold nights, cool days, and high mountains. Tibet with yaks and sheep. Tibet with Tibetans. Tibetan mastiffs. Tibetan foxes. Tibetan snow lions. Tibetan salt. In Tibet there are little blue flowers and something like mole/prairie dogs. In Tibet there are dharma practitioners who really mean it. Tibet has piles of rocks with prayers. Tibet is crowded with electricity wires. Tibet is full of Chinese people. Tibet has buses and motorcycles. Tibet has a lot of mud. Tibetan rivers drown people who cannot swim, and most Tibetans cannot swim. Tibet is full of merchants selling everything and especially cordyceps and dzi. Tibet has butchers who sell meat. Tibet has many monasteries. Tibet has snow. Tibet is very high up. Tibet is very bright. Tibet has night life. Tibetans like horses. Tibetans LOVE to sing. Some Tibetans are great dancers. Some Tibetans might cut your thumb off. Some Tibetans never give a good deal. Tibetans eat butter till it kills them. Tibetans don't like to bathe much. Tibetans have bad knees. Tibetans may have golden or rotten teeth. Tibetans pray a lot. Tibetans are very studious, some of them. Tibetans are very meticulous. Tibetans won't break their backs to scrub the floor. Tibetans will eat for entertainment. Tibetans snore. Tibetans keep secrets well. Tibetans gossip so much. Tibetans can flirt! Tibetans get serious.

Talkie No.2

Woodstock, NY—home by divine command.

expand expand
expand expand expand expand
expand expand expand expand
expand expand expand expand
expand expand expand expand
expand expand expand

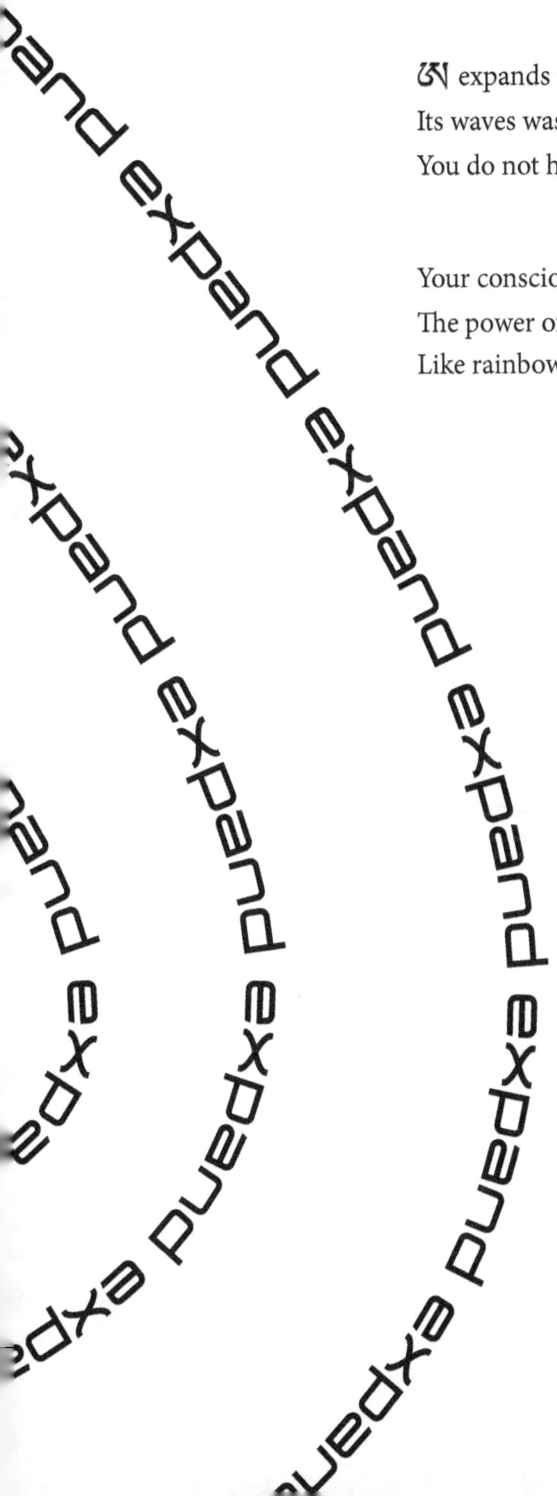
expand expand expand expand
expand expand expand
expand expand

ཨ། expands throughout space
Its waves wash through you
You do not have a body

Your consciousness alone experiences
The power of ཨ།
Like rainbow air

so endlessly hovering slightly breathing but unignorable mining down for it for
it holds the shape of it couldn't stop it once it started out of hand a bit surly
picture another bunt cake or hanging watching by the trees they were murderous
came to see like disembodied eyes in the dark they were watching it so.....so

"could've been a doctor" sign-holder says twirling into the setting skies p
erhaps he had some place to be an enemy landscape so similar to ho
me different stores and language but mirror-reflected people populate
the township similar enough floral home dresses and slipper sandals too

bury me any way you like - there are no further requests hold
your fire soldier tender meat smells good coffee break for the
lovers endlessly brewing and if you live you will need to
wash clothes and find shelter and food-stuffs like stuffing

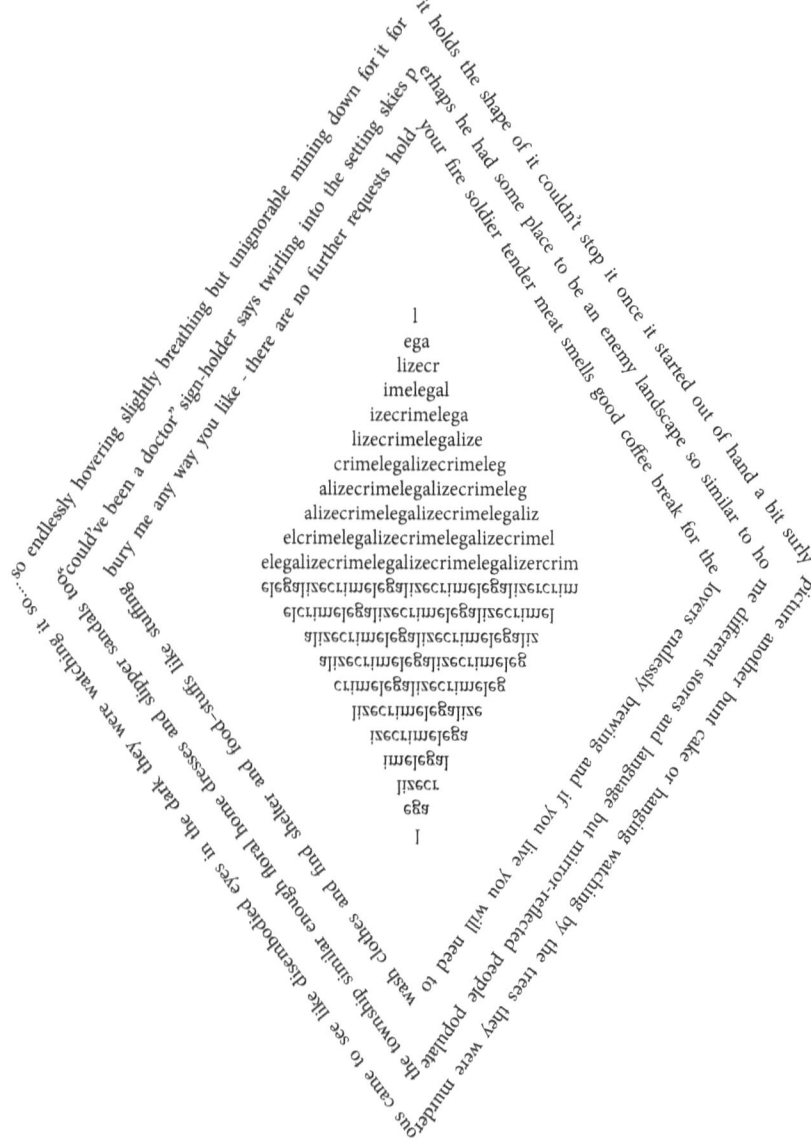

l
ega
lizecr
imelegal
izecrimelega
lizecrimelegalize
crimelegalizecrimeleg
alizecrimelegalizecrimeleg
alizecrimelegalizecrimelegaliz
elcrimelegalizecrimelegalizecrimel
elegalizecrimelegalizecrimelegalizercrim
elegalizecrimelegalizecrimelegalizercrim
elcrimelegalizecrimelegalizecrimel
alizecrimelegalizecrimelegaliz
alizecrimelegalizecrimeleg
crimelegalizecrimeleg
lizecrimelegalize
izecrimelega
imelegal
lizecr
ega
l

Diamond Poem is the size of a five-story building
suspended in air at the end of a city street
lined with stores and homes

It's as if no one sees it
It is thin, the letters having no width but are black in color
It slightly rotates forward back and side to side, slowly

You approach it with awe
canned drink in hand
change in pocket

Your chin drops a ¼ inch
Oddly it doesn't shine or glow
Just hovers in day light

Driveway

I saw her in the driveway
She was yelling
Yelling at her money
She was yelling at her money
Like a
Like a crazy person
She was
Yelling at her money in the driveway
With her hair falling out
Or onto her fur coat
Yelling with her hair falling out or onto
Her fur lined coat sleeve
Holding some bills
In the driveway
She was yelling
Yelling at her money
Right next to
My car

Do I exist if I don;t spend money?
Do I exist if I don't spend money?

Sometimes I don't feel real if I don't spend money.
If I don't buyn e anything, what am I?

No records. Nrecrds N r ecrds NO RECORDS NO RECORDSNORECORDS N O R E C O R D S
MONEY MAKE IT SPEND IT RECORD MONEY MAKE IT SPEND IT RECORD MONEY
NO MONEY NO RECORD NO MONEY NO RECORD NO MONEY NO RECORD NO MONEY NO RECORD
ya know
maybe I'm crazy, but it unhhh seems to mee that without money no one will
record, keep, store, care about shit NO MONEY NO TIME NO.
So if you don't buy something and give me some of thatt sweet sweet moola
you can be gone - gone to the wind, gone to the fire, gone to the dogs I DON'T CARE
GET OFF MY STEPS, NOW.

I feel like I should buy something... I feel the itch to spend some..

what I spend. valued for what I spend. "Spending Power" got to have that...

Sometimes I don;t feel real if I don't spend money. Maybe I'm...
Maybe I'm sick? made myself sick.. still I.. I feel like I gotta
Make it. Spend it. Be alive.

Make it. spend it. Be alive.
Make and spend and look alive
You gotta make it baby look alive
Don't spend your nights and days inside
Resorts, malls, SUVs, everything you see omn TV.

Make it so you stay alive
Spend it like you're gunna die
Don't just sit and stay inside
Spend your paycheck in a night!

$ $$ $ $ $

(ching cha-ching ching ching ching)

"Capitalist Anxieties" C. Lama 2020

H E L P

I've fallen out of the system

And I don't exist.

My body is not proof of my identity.

I have fallen out of the system

And I can't get back in.

No birth certificate

No social security card
No license; never had a car
No shelter, no storage
No money
No records
    I can't get them. . .no money

T o ta l Zerö C .Lam

Death and Shopping: A Tripart Series

I ordered an item on ebay,
but the seller is dead.
How can he/she refund me
if they are dead?
Help me, ebay.

She died two weeks ago.
As of today, seventeen packages
have arrived in her name.
what if they fill up the entire lobby?
How will we reach the elevator?
When will the concierge dispose of them?
Shall we tunnel, gondola to the staircase,
sailing through a somber sea of packages?

I have died,
but I'm waiting for my order.
I want to see it arrive.
I sincerely hope someone unboxes it.
I will follow it wherever it may go,
to my sister's house, to the trash, the dump.
I will haunt the dump that houses my order.
I will join it beneath the garbage mountain,
laying still and content.

All My Pursuits

All my pursuits have been selfish.

~~I worked hard to improve my skills in writing and translation.~~

~~I denied going to Harvard to avoid causing financial strain on my family.~~

~~I "studied" the Buddha Dharma.~~

~~I wrote and performed many songs.~~

~~I drew comics that depicted great hardships in life.~~

~~I sewed my sister a custom shirt to her liking.~~

~~I always remembered to give my parents gifts.~~

~~I kept in touch with old friends.~~

~~Once I worked all night on a diagram to assist my spiritual community.~~

~~I was patient while suffering depression.~~

~~I encouraged, supported and celebrated my colleagues.~~

~~I gave money to what I deemed worthy causes.~~

Talkie No.3

While in voluntary confinement, I thought...

Bedside Viewer

The dead moth whispers to me.
its tomb is the cloth crevice-catcher I affixed to the wall
and wood-panel lining the side of my bed.
It speaks not of its short and monotonous life,
but asks if the subbed version of the latest episode is up yet.
I tell it to be patient.

And I Accept That

I was sick of reading other people's short stories that took too long to get to the point. I was looking for words like "HIV" to pop out and grab my attention; sadly, they never came.

There are Korean pop stars who wear shoulder pads far too large for their frames so shamelessly and deliberately that no one cares to comment.

I watched the slender man fall to the floor in his clumsy trademark fashion, hysterical while his "associates" looked on, also hysterical.

His eyes were upturned crescent moons with black curves where his lashes met. He was beautiful, and he made it that way through a series of surgeries.

I have, of late, been quite obsessed with viewing before and after plastic surgery images.

Yes, their faces and bodies may have changed, but they're still the same insecure people they always were.

English grammar is breaking down, and I'm not helping, I know. I feel as if I should care more...

These are the unspoken ravings of a human who thinks too much and has no one to talk to.

I think I'm going blind in my right eye. There seems to be a white spot that obstructs my vision in a place I've noticed many times now.

As for my hearing, I am certain I'm losing it. Everything falls apart, and I accept that.

Bell of Cultivation

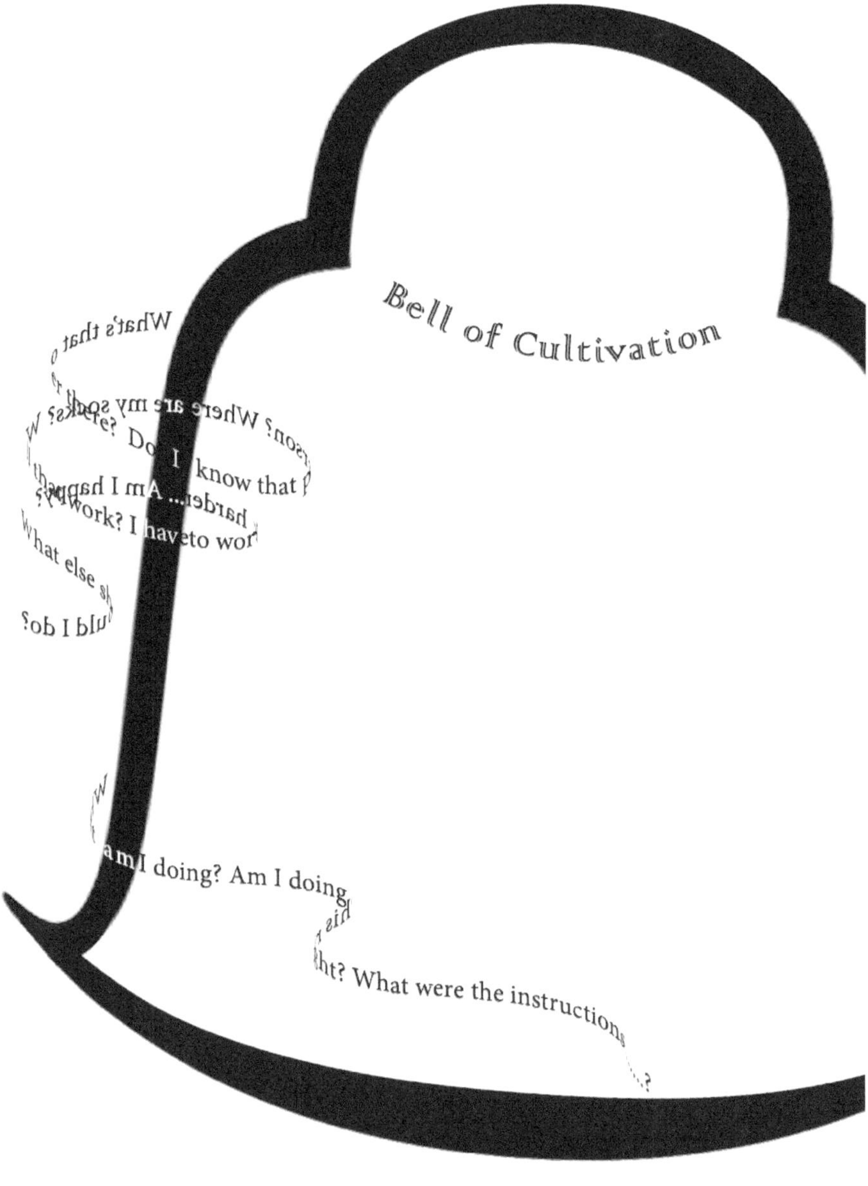
What's that
Where are my socks?
Where? Do I know that
Am I happy?
harder...
work? I have to work
What else should I do?
am I doing? Am I doing this right? What were the instructions...?

Bell of Cultivation

I don't know what I'm doing, Mary thinks.
Lama said look at the nature of mind, not the thoughts.

My mind has a nature?

Outside the window of her safe and warm retreat house,
the leaves rise with the wind.

Mary drinks tea and breathes.
There is no one else in the house.
Rose left four days ago, and she never missed company so much.
Nothing left but herself and her mind now.
That and Lama's instructions, like a riddle.

Up the stairs. Down the stairs.
The patch of wall opposite the toilet.
The carpeted shrine room and the light of the butter lamp.
Hushed nights and quiet afternoons.

Mary grates cheese to make quesadillas.
There's no hope of sour cream.
She has no car. She is stranded.
She can get food from the monastery that is nearby.
There is a path through the woods.

I'll go tomorrow for tomatoes and rice.
I wonder if Wangchen will be working in the kitchen.
I'm excited to see anyone...

Back up the stairs to the shrine room, to her corner.
There she sits, hour after hour, practicing, reciting, visualizing.
Until nighttime, she sits with crossed legs, making as much as a dent
in her negative habitual patterns as silk wiping an iron bell.

***

The camouflage bark of the sycamore trees in Prospect Park.
Looking up to see the underside of her friend's breasts.
Laying on top of a wooden picnic table, 18 years old.
Thoughts like these flash, one after the other.

Not to resist the thoughts, but not to indulge them.
Let them be. Just sit.
Whatever arises, just sit.
Waking up after a drunken night next to some body.
Disappointing her professor by writing a bad essay—these thoughts make her twitch.

***

Let them go. Not the time for engaging.
Her task is to sit and sit only.
That means NOT planning, reminiscing, longing or dozing off.
That means being awake and aware of her mind.
Just be with the mind.

Who knew it would be so difficult?
Morning to night, be with the mind.
"Are you crazy?" her friend asked. "Meditation's the *last* thing I need."
But she doesn't feel that way...

***

A silent living room, dark with no lights on.
Evening falls like a hush on the silent house.
"Nothing" she thinks. "Nothing here...just me...and who am I?"
"If I walk, am I real? Is that proof enough?"
"If I eat I must be real because I made something disappear..."
Assumptions.

Twice a month she meets with her teacher.
She never knows what to say.
Thankfully, he knows what to ask.
She only has to respond honestly, and he knows how to instruct her.
"Doing good" he would say, and smile.
Her heart never felt more warm.

***

Keeping track of the days, though time loses meaning.
She is entering the third month.
Cream of potatoes and parsley linger on her tongue as she
raises it to her palate.
"That gives saliva a place to flow" said Pema, the last retreatant
before flying away.

Sitting at the dining table,
listening to water drop in the sink.
Take a sip of water.
Know you're taking a sip of water.
She sees herself in a small cottage, somewhere in New Hampshire,
praying there, seated on a cushion,
maybe with a dog…
Oh no! I left my water drinking!

For three seconds she was in a dream cottage,
and NOT in the retreat house with full awareness.

"It happens so swiftly—so swiftly!" she thinks,
and resolves not to let her mind slip away from her awareness for the rest
of the night.

After closing the last session of the day,
after the last dedication,
she feels the urge to take a walk.
Outside it's brisk with the sun's red glow.
Her heart feels still, her stomach settled.
The scent of fallen leaves fills the air.
What a blessing to be alive.

Cool prayer beads and their roundness
hang from her hand by her hip.
Thumbing each bead with a wish,
she takes a step and another.
Walking down the private road till it meets the main road.
Turning and walking back tenderly.

TRIFECTA

tam tam tam tam tam
hrih hrih hrih hrih hrih
dhi dhi dhi dhi dhi dhi

Tibetan Concrete Poetry Annotations

"Trifecta" displays three sets of brackets that are closed, forming what appears to be containers or temples. These bracket temples contain the English phonetic equivalent of Tibetan seed syllables that represent the aural form of the deity. *Tam* is the seed syllable of Āryā Tārā who is associated with swift activity. *Hrih* is the seed syllable of Amitabha and Avalokiteśvara and is associated with compassion. *Dhi* is the seed syllable of Mañjuśrī and is associated with wisdom. The recitation of these syllables is believed to impart their blessing.

"Soaring Bodies" depicts the Tibetan seed syllable *Om* that represents the enlightened body of the Buddha. Here we see them floating out of open brackets composed of Tibetan *U-gur* or "title tents." They are used to frame titles of works, and in this piece they part, allowing the *Om*s to soar up and out. *See p.65.*

"Peeking Om" presents a sea of temples with *Om*s peeking out, but only partly. This forms a hypnotic yet a-symmetrical design that resembles flower petals, or alternatively, flames of fire. *See p.76.*

She 1

Ran to the door

She, wearing spotted dress, flushed cheeks, wild eyes

Looks outside

Kwak

She 2

She walks in with a bone structure I've never seen before.

She 3

She didn't say.

Her life; her plans.

Turned a profile,

and didn't say.

When speaking was deemed defiant
I remained silent.

Now I have trouble speaking.
Now I have trouble speaking right.

I tremble.
I tick.

When will I be able to speak fluidly?
Am I dumb?

When I cannot speak
there is nothing I can do.

Maybe don't look;
____ __ ____.

Untitled
C. Lama

He could
        n't

He couldn't tell the

            tell the di

He couldn't tell the difference of

                                    course

When sh
   When shhhh
       When she asked him
                asked him
                asked him "What

                asked him "What have

                "What have I

                            done?"

"The Pronoun for woman Starts with 'Be quiet'"

shhh Lama 2020

...How to love and leave a man...How to love and leave a man...How to love and leave a man...How to love and leave a man...How to love and leave a man...How to

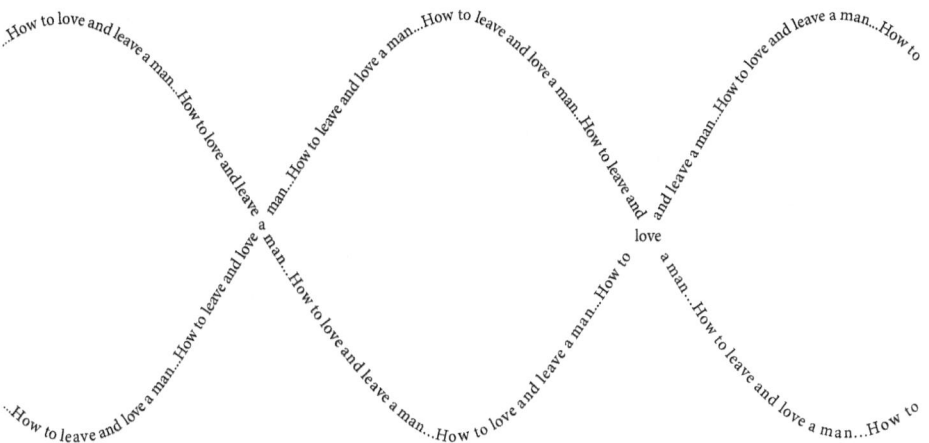

...How to leave and love a man...How to leave and love a man...How to leave and love a man...How to leave and love a man...How to leave and love a man...How to

Thrill

The little things.
You sharing my glass
In public.

Fore/Back

Since I wanted to get hit by a car, I moved to NYC.

Since she wanted to be a widow, she married an important person.

Since they wanted caregivers, they had children.

Since she wanted to be caught, she left evidence.

Since he wanted to be stopped, he persisted.

Since she wanted to be fired, she did nothing.

Since I wanted to have chipped nails, I painted them.

It's Your Turn, Oxana.

If I leave her alone, what does she do?
(I watch)

If I move too fast I lose my shoes.

Corpus Christi!

Corpus Christi!

Corpus Christi?
Corpus Christi!

Make narrative sense!
Make narrative sense!

flambang!

FLAMBANG.

Stacker 1958

C. Lama 2020

ding dong my dear
H
o bifur..
w dping my dear
t
o
ding ding ding dear c r b
e a i
t e sng png mmdr f
u
a r
c
timai mur reer n e ding dong my dear dear a.
dika rika rurr e .
d dilla fing bir
ding
dikka rur rurr
ted dear
whisper fields
in

lamplight

b
f i
s r u
e c
hc
n a t a
e
r d
b
r
c n a
s e h
my dear

ding
i t kururu ruhh?

dddddrrrrruuuuuuu

"at the do
or" C. Lama 2020

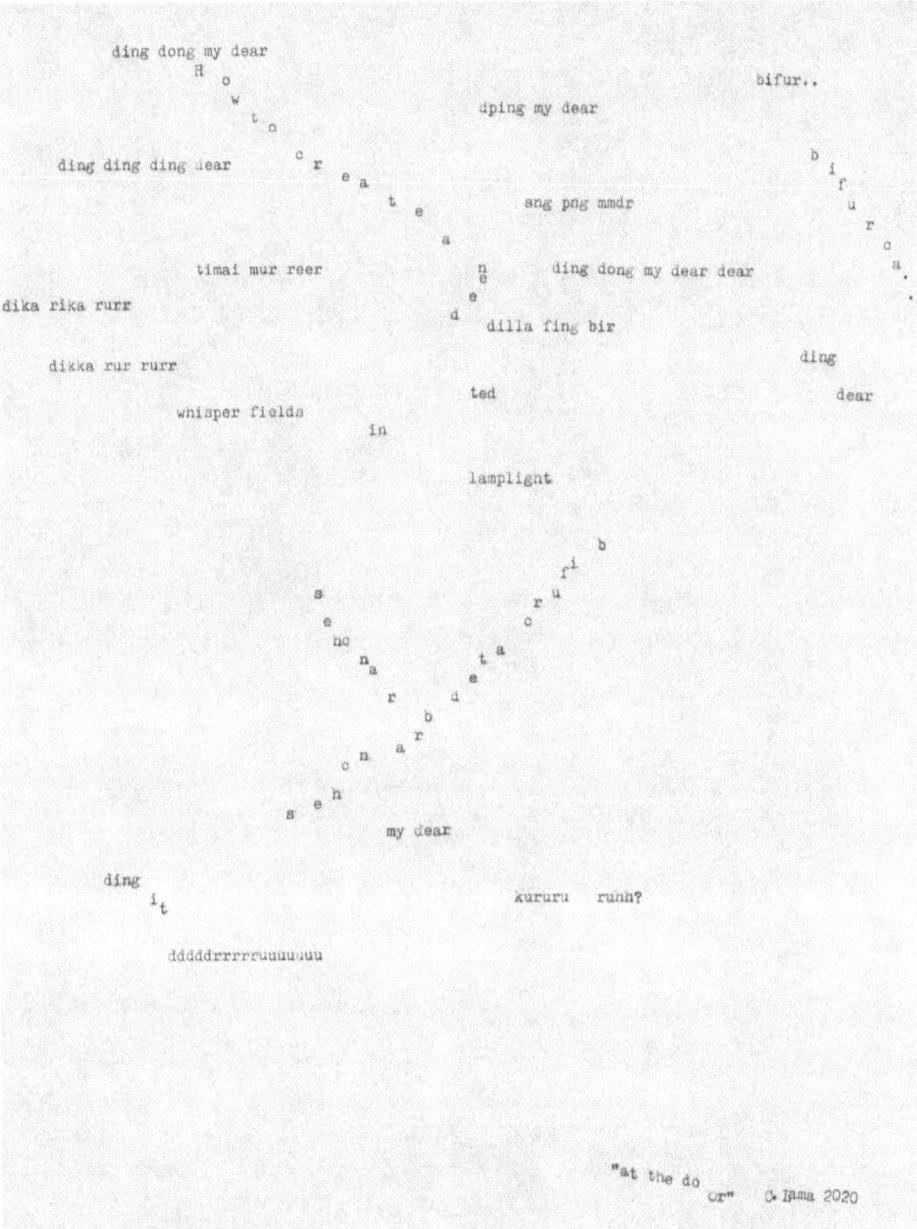

a blue bird, house and chisel

head on desk, like beheaded
I have neither the skill nor patience
for typewriters
Come have some tea instead
steep now, my love   steep

enraged by my tools
"process" frustrates me

open top so I can see all the keys
change my chair
analysts / restless
a. dig
a dig for meaning

Why does sense have to lead me?

even on this gray joyless day?
milkless   milkless   milkless

living: what I'm doing
When you think of trees,
is it an Oak, Elm, Cedar?
my keys look like caramel, and now
I want some
earthen
declassified
I may plumb ya boy
Who's to say?
wiissshhaaahhaaa

it breaks/broken/to break/broke
eateateateateateateateat eateateateateat
She
wasn't   She wouldn't   here? What now?
W

lue bird, hov
ad on desk, l
e neither the
or typewriters
me have some
eep now, my l
aged by my too
"proce
n top so I car
ange my chair
analy
dig
a dig for
y does sense
en on this gra
kless milkl
ving: what I'm
When you
is it
my keys look
I want s
ea
I may plumb
Who's
wiiss
it breaks/br
eateateateateat
She wasn't S

se and chis
ike behead
skill nor
tea insteac
ove steep
ols
ss" frustrat
see all th
sts / restle
meaning
have to lead
y joyless da
ess milkle
doing
think of tre
n Oak, Elm,
ike caramel,
ome
rthen
declass
ya boy
to say?
shhaaahhaaa
oken/to breal
teateateateat
he wouldn't
W

ei
d
patience
i
tes me
e keys
ss
me?
y?
ss
es,
Cedar?
and now
ified
/broke
eateateateateat
here? What now?

I let the letters

T H E R E S A H A K K Y U N G C H A

K A R M A C H I M E C H O D O N L A M A

Swim free

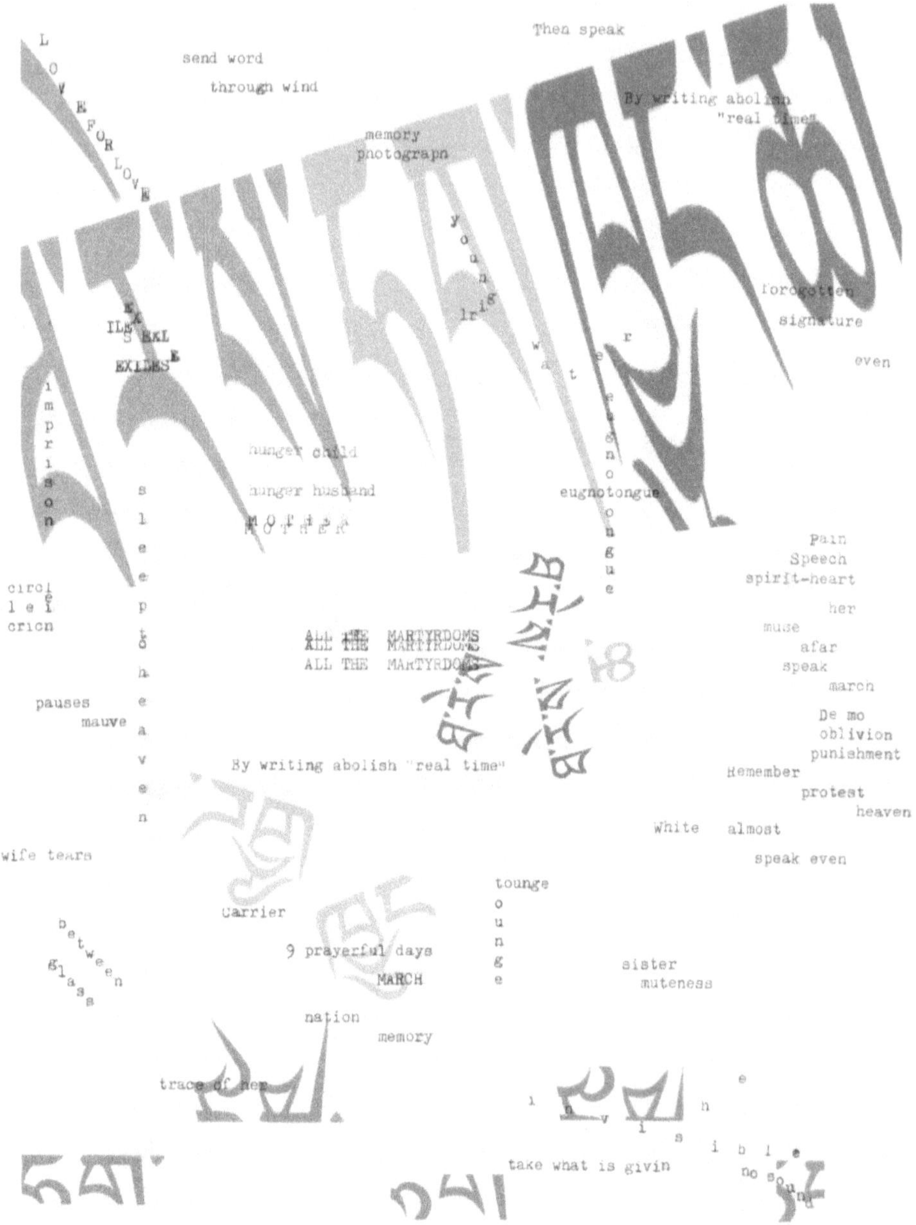
Then speak
send word
through wind
By writing abolish
"real time"
memory
photograph
LOVE FOR LOVE
young
forgotten
signature
even
EXILES
imprison
water
hunger child
hunger husband
eugnotongue
MOTHER
sleep to heaven
pain
Speech
spirit-heart
her
muse
afar
speak
march
ALL THE MARTYRDOMS
ALL THE MARTYRDOMS
ALL THE MARTYRDOMS
pauses
mauve
De mo
oblivion
punishment
By writing abolish "real time"
Remember
protest
heaven
White
almost
wife tears
speak even
tounge
Carrier
between glass
9 prayerful days
MARCH
sister
muteness
nation
memory
trace of her
invisible
take what is givin
no sound

RETURN / ཕྱིར་ལོག།

Like coal in snow

གངས་ནང་པའི་སོལ་བ་ནང་བཞིན།

གང་ཡང་མ་སྤྲད་པས་སོང་
མ་བྱུང་།

You didn't leave us
with nothing

Saw it come together

གཅིག་ཏུ་འདུས་པ་མཐོང་སོང་།

ཁྱེད་ཀྱི་བྱ་བ་མཐོང་།

Saw you do it

Each page a swan

ངོ་ཤོག་རེ་རེ་ངང་པ།

སྨུག་པའི་ལོ་རྒྱུས།

Mist narrative

My wish to engulf you

ཁྱེད་རང་ཁྱུར་མིད་གཏོང་བའི་རེ་བ།

གཉིས་ཀྱིས་བྲག་གཡང་ནས་ལྷུང་།
ཤུགས་གཡར་བ་ཆེད་དུ་
ས་འོག་ཏུ་བཏང་ཆོག

Two falling off a cliff
allowed underground
to lend strength

milk milk milk milk milk milk milk
milk milk milk milk milk milk milk
milk milk milk milk milk milk milk
milk milk milk milk milk milk milk milk

k milk milk milk milk

ilk milk milk milk milk

milk milk milk milk

milk milk milk milk milk milk milk milk milk mi

ilk milk milk mi

Talkie No. 4

I fell into a valley of grapefruits

O yes

milk milk milk milk milk milk mil

milk milk milk milk milk milk mil

milk milk milk milk milk mi

ilk milk milk milk mil

WINDOW PIECE

Look at a window as if it's looking at you.

2020 spring

POKE PIECE

Poke every person you see for a week.

2020 spring

FISH NAME PIECE

Imagine your body is filled with fishes and water.
Count the fishes and make that number your middle name.

2020 spring

TIME PIECE

1. Think of time.
2. Don't think.
3. Think.

2020 spring

ROSE PIECE

Buy one red rose.
Rub it on your face as much as you like.
Eat a petal.
Put four petals in water.
Wait two hours.
Drink the rose petal water.

2020 spring

MATH PIECE

Read a mathematical equation out loud and call it a poem.

2020 spring

Kick Box

Find a box large enough to fit a human.
Have the consenting person enter the box.
Let them remain there alone in silence for 15 minutes.
Any time after 15 minutes allow observers to approach the box.
Tell them nothing, save "You may do anything you'd like to the box."
Observers may interact with the box any way they like.
They may not use weapons or touch the box with anything but their bodies.
They have 5 minutes with the box. The person within the box must be over 18.

(Inspired by Walter De-Maria)

PENCIL PIECE

Shout the first word that comes to your mind.
Hold a pencil over paper and prepare yourself to write an entire book about it.
Break the pencil.
Abandon the project.

2020 spring

CUMIN PIECE

Sprinkle cumin into the air.
Never sweep it up.

2020 spring

SUNLIGHT PIECE

Stand in sunlight, eating sunlight.

2020 spring

My existence with you is beautiful. By that I mean sunshine rain in tokyo. Two bright green tree frogs. A warm cup of cocoa. You bring me assorted pastries from which I will grow fat and happy

I'm beset with traditional concerns like will our family's lineage protector curse me if I live with a man out of wedlock? Will I give birth to a demon if I make love in the morning or during a

thunderstorm? Will I ever repay my parents' kindness? Is the only loyalty to be a spinster? As if I heard your eyes lift to meet me

Listening to your dream job over and over. You sleep on the snore bed when I snore. You cook! Who cooks?! I cook? In the electric

lamp light praying for my father's good health. For his health.

The humbleness of a new family and warm pie from the oven.

Talkie No.5

JAPAN JAPAN JAPAN JAPAN JAPAN JAPAN JAPAN JAPAN JAPAN JAPAN JAPAN
JAPAN JAPAN JAPAN JAPAN JAPAN JAPAN JAPAN JAPAN JAPAN JAPAN JAPAN
JAPAN JAPAN JAPAN JAPAN JAPAN JAPAN JAPAN JAPAN JAPAN JAPAN JAPAN
JAPAN JAPAN JAPAN JAPAN JAPAN JAPAN JAPAN JAPAN JAPAN JAPAN JAPAN
JAPAN JAPAN JAPAN JAPAN JAPAN JAPAN JAPAN JAPAN JAPAN JAPAN JAPAN
JAPAN JAPAN JAPAN JAPAN JAPAN JAPAN JAPAN JAPAN JAPAN JAPAN JAPAN
JAPAN JAPAN JAPAN JAPAN JAPAN JAPAN JAPAN JAPAN JAPAN JAPAN JAPAN
JAPAN JAPAN JAPAN JAPAN JAPAN JAPAN JAPAN JAPAN JAPAN JAPAN JAPAN
JAPAN JAPAN JAPAN JAPAN JAPAN JAPAN JAPAN JAPAN JAPAN JAPAN JAPAN
JAPAN JAPAN JAPAN JAPAN JAPAN JAPAN JAPAN JAPAN JAPAN JAPAN JAPAN
JAPAN JAPAN JAPAN JAPAN JAPAN JAPAN JAPAN JAPAN JAPAN JAPAN JAPAN
JAPAN JAPAN JAPAN JAPAN JAPAN JAPAN JAPAN JAPAN JAPAN JAPAN JAPAN
JAPAN JAPAN JAPAN JAPAN JAPAN JAPAN JAPAN JAPAN JAPAN JAPAN JAPAN
JAPAN JAPAN JAPAN JAPAN JAPAN JAPAN JAPAN JAPAN JAPAN JAPAN JAPAN
JAPAN JAPAN JAPAN JAPAN JAPAN JAPAN JAPAN JAPAN JAPAN JAPAN JAPAN
JAPAN JAPAN JAPAN JAPAN JAPAN JAPAN JAPAN JAPAN JAPAN JAPAN JAPAN
JAPAN JAPAN JAPAN JAPAN JAPAN JAPAN JAPAN JAPAN JAPAN JAPAN JAPAN
JAPAN JAPAN JAPAN JAPAN JAPAN JAPAN
JAPAN JAPAN JAPAN JAPANOPHILES UNITE JAPAN JAPAN JAPAN
JAPAN JAPAN JAPAN JAPAN JAPAN JAPAN
JAPAN JAPAN JAPAN JAPAN JAPAN JAPAN JAPAN JAPAN JAPAN JAPAN JAPAN
JAPAN JAPAN JAPAN JAPAN JAPAN JAPAN JAPAN JAPAN JAPAN JAPAN JAPAN
JAPAN JAPAN JAPAN JAPAN JAPAN JAPAN JAPAN JAPAN JAPAN JAPAN JAPAN
JAPAN JAPAN JAPAN JAPAN JAPAN JAPAN JAPAN JAPAN JAPAN JAPAN JAPAN
JAPAN JAPAN JAPAN JAPAN JAPAN JAPAN JAPAN JAPAN JAPAN JAPAN JAPAN
JAPAN JAPAN JAPAN JAPAN JAPAN JAPAN JAPAN JAPAN JAPAN JAPAN JAPAN
JAPAN JAPAN JAPAN JAPAN JAPAN JAPAN JAPAN JAPAN JAPAN JAPAN JAPAN
JAPAN JAPAN JAPAN JAPAN JAPAN JAPAN JAPAN JAPAN JAPAN JAPAN JAPAN
JAPAN JAPAN JAPAN JAPAN JAPAN JAPAN JAPAN JAPAN JAPAN JAPAN JAPAN
JAPAN JAPAN JAPAN JAPAN JAPAN JAPAN JAPAN JAPAN JAPAN JAPAN JAPAN
JAPAN JAPAN JAPAN JAPAN JAPAN JAPAN JAPAN JAPAN JAPAN JAPAN JAPAN
JAPAN JAPAN JAPAN JAPAN JAPAN JAPAN JAPAN JAPAN JAPAN JAPAN JAPAN
JAPAN JAPAN JAPAN JAPAN JAPAN JAPAN JAPAN JAPAN JAPAN JAPAN JAPAN
JAPAN JAPAN JAPAN JAPAN JAPAN JAPAN JAPAN JAPAN JAPAN JAPAN JAPAN
JAPAN JAPAN JAPAN JAPAN JAPAN JAPAN JAPAN JAPAN JAPAN JAPAN JAPAN
JAPAN JAPAN JAPAN JAPAN JAPAN JAPAN JAPAN JAPAN JAPAN JAPAN JAPAN
JAPAN JAPAN JAPAN JAPAN JAPAN JAPAN JAPAN JAPAN JAPAN JAPAN JAPAN
JAPAN JAPAN JAPAN JAPAN JAPAN JAPAN JAPAN JAPAN JAPAN JAPAN JAPAN
JAPAN JAPAN JAPAN JAPAN JAPAN JAPAN JAPAN JAPAN JAPAN JAPAN JAPAN
JAPAN JAPAN JAPAN JAPAN JAPAN JAPAN JAPAN JAPAN JAPAN JAPAN JAPAN
JAPAN JAPAN JAPAN JAPAN JAPAN JAPAN JAPAN JAPAN JAPAN JAPAN JAPAN
JAPAN JAPAN JAPAN JAPAN JAPAN JAPAN JAPAN JAPAN JAPAN JAPAN JAPAN
JAPAN JAPAN JAPAN JAPAN JAPAN JAPAN JAPAN JAPAN JAPAN JAPAN JAPAN
JAPAN JAPAN JAPAN JAPAN JAPAN JAPAN JAPAN JAPAN JAPAN JAPAN JAPAN

Morning Snow

There is something she won't forgive him
It makes her fly off her seat
Snow weighs down the pine tree branches
Moment to moment wet chunks fall
Keeping her from her sadness

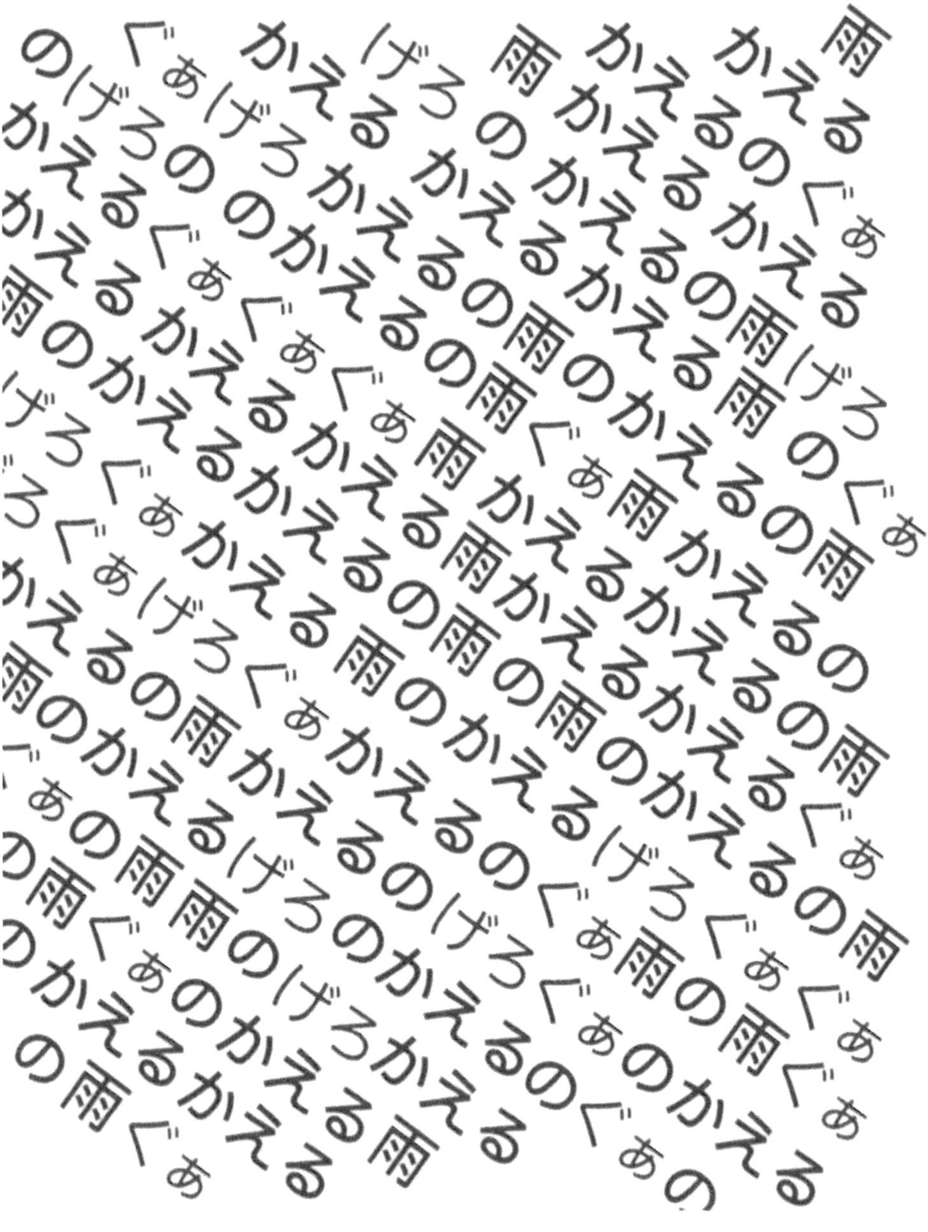
雨
かえる
かえるのじぁ

Frog-rain

Kaeru no ame

かえるの雨

げろ

gero

ぐわ

gwa

ribbit/puke

ribbit

o
Oyo

h e t t h e r e m o e r
sandsaI realizsedldit iNwgas her wish.

x t e
nEoiYesL!ft

h e t t h e r e m o d e r
asnd IsarealizedsitlwasihnegR wish.

e x t e t
noiYelsf!

/\\/p/\\/oy/\\/y/\\/o/\\/p/\\/oy/\\/y/\\/o

m i e e d
ay fflacNelisft

m a e m
letkterSy perky!

i m
stlhe margins

i V e
cGolor!ussome

t e e i a i r o v
t e e i a i r o v
a hhd re v e r hhh e r e a o o e r
anndreverssyywwhereaIlllll1lookk.:rmmyyllıffee

Ode to Sumō

Any floating pillar god,
any cold black turtle
would bless the earthen dōhyo
supposing the rikishi are noble

Suppose it is January
Suppose no city but Tokyo
Supposing that the yokozuna
are able-bodied and willing

As well as the ozeki,
supposing Asanoyama, Enho, Ishiura,
and every stable master
were gathered all together

Suppose a sea of sponsors,
Waving many colored banners,
and supposing that the gyōgi
looks like a pile of grapes

Supposing strong water,
clean salt and clenched fists,
Suppose a rush of bodies,
a clap of thunder

Sumō!

This poem depicts the profile
of the chest and stomach
of the greatest sumō wrestler to date,
Hakuhō Shō. (Try squinting your eyes.)

du
st
collecting contest

We will

~~meet~~ GATHER

8 on the 8th 88

88 8
8 8 88 8 8 8 8 8
8 9 8 8
8 8 8 98 8 8 8
8 8 8
8 8 8 8 8 8 8 u8
8 8 8 8 8 8 8 8 8 8 8 8 8
8 8 8 8 8 8 8 8 8 8 8 8
8 888 8 8 8 8 8 8
8 8 8 8 8 8 8 8 8 8 8 8 8 8
8 8 8 8 8 8 8 8 8 8
8 8 8 8 8 8 8 8
8 8 8 8
8 8 8 8 8 8
8 8 8 8 8 8 8 8
8 8 8 8
8 8 8 8
8 8
8 8
8 8 8 8 8 8

La Salute Mentale

My friend _______ took a walk to

her bed, and moaned. "Don't cry"
said the fan. "What did I tell
you about shutting up?" yawned
the cat. Two eggs shivered in
the fridge, awaiting their

City Path

Since life is so hectic, I'
ll take peace wherever I can get it.

Log is a Bench

I go to the woods and look for someone to fall in love with

I forget that I'm already in love

read three pages of words in the setting sun, more for the light than the meaning

Biweekly Walk

On my way home
I see no one...

Unable to look at people
I see feet for faces

Is it ok to exist like this?

The cold biting through my jacket

I/Other

Since I have anger issues, I think other people have anger issues.

The Braggart

Asking an artist to promote is like asking them to brag.

Bragging undoes decency.

Train Tracks

To avoid people, I walk so close to the wall I scrape my ear.

What's my problem?

Train tracks criss-cross this country,
bringing with them many stories.

Judger

I think my lover thinks I know he's judging me.

(Seen on Youtube
Overweight older man tells healthy young man not to be self effacing, but pompus.)

Phenomena

As the projects pile up,
the ceiling becomes more fascinating

Tea Cup Full One

His cup me to give did.

How much drink if my own choice.

People all to mouth full a give if, tea this enough gi will.

Salt strike did ey?

His friend my stomach top on puke did.

By me tissue to get go did.

Wipe if although, little left was.

Bathroom to go, difficult.

One day gi in to,

Food times three makes gi does.

Me to profit very got did.

Quietly-ly laugh laugh gi do.

Welcome_to_the_waking_world_Email=great_stress_Hw_am_I_nt_myel_How_am_I_not_the_summer_breeze?____
Don't_like_watching_movies_too_long_mmmaaaaaannn sittin around_waiting_on_water_to_boil_I'm
an_asshole_grieving_over_tree_death_peed_on_by_an air_conditioner_I_had_that_
talk_with_myself_a_long_time_ago_(indistinct_chatter)_ferrying_messages between_blood_between_farts
You_who_play_the_accordian_of_my_heart_in_#%&#_me asure_for_rupture_itself_
Still_waiting_on_the_marinara_from_the_sea_bird_ of_ South_ Car lina*_Will_diners_lose_
their*warm_fuzzy_feeling_when_waitresses_are_repl aced_with_RO BOTS ????_Release_me_Genna_()____
Welcome_to_the_perishing_world*I_have_4_badminton_rackets when ever I 'm_inside_I_wish_I_was_ou
When_Email======great_stress_Wo_m_I_ot_msl?_Welcome live being possessing greater_and_lesser_warmth*__
Welcome_cackeling_hags_unite!_lc...ccccccuve hal & and_harmless_we_swears_i
My_To_Don't_Note_as_my_only_Compass-Lord-&-Savior_ battling_a_fragrant_monster_made_of_basil_she_st
ess es_and stresses_some more doing_less_good_ than a corpse the strength_of_slumber_to_abate_t
e_ waking_world_ ma

Give_me_waking_world_ma_Tak
me_here/there_startled_backward_3_lives_ Genji a_bla re_ color ful_flowers pouches_and_fake
flowers_occupied_her_waking_life_Bitter_ melon_ head Every spine bending_bending6_We_live_on
this_strange_earth_where_everything_falls_ to_ the_ ground My_body_falls_My_body_falls_Play_
where_a_mute_girl_has_the_performance_of_ her life_ in_ the_ woods_before_an_audience_of
trees_Slicing_time_like_pie_

WOVEN WORDS

WOVEN WORDS

Two catches

c a u g h t

each other

My sweetheart is an invitation to nap

There was blue and there was white and there was dark blue fading to light

Wearing an outfit like your parents

With limbs like that, his DNA must have thought there was all the space in the world

She had a stroke - it was perfect. Text book symptoms, I'm not surprised. It's just what I'd expect of Evelyn.

told you it looked good on you

The sun passes us who are doing this

She said it smells like a body bag in here. What does that smell like?

and that in our little North facing room

Gratitude = Lerned Behavior

Entr

Matrix

I'm grateful for bacon but I don't want to offend the vegetarians and vegans. I'm grateful for bacon but I don't want to offend the vegetarians and veg

I'm grateful for hot water turned warm and enjoyable in the bathtub. I'm grateful for hot water turned warm and enjoyable in the bathtub I'm grateful

Grateful you're still there when I part from your body to write these notes. I'm grateful you're still there when I part from your body to write these notes

I'm grateful for 1 AM, the time for thinkers. I'm grateful for 1 AM, the time for thinkers. I'm grateful for 1 AM, the time for thinkers. I'm grateful for

For the kind people I ignore. For the kind people I ignore. For the kind people I ignore. For the kind people I ignore. For the kind people I ignore. F

Grateful for my basil plant that grows like a sapling and for the pesto of its juices. Grateful for my basil plant that grows like a sapling and for the pes

Grateful I no longer need to type: dictation. Grateful I no longer need to type: dictation. Grateful I no longer need to type: dictation. Grateful I no lo

I'm grateful for the rain and the life it brings. I'm grateful for the rain and the growth it supports. Grateful for the earth and the growth it supports.

Grateful for the earth and the growth it supports. Grateful for the earth and the life it brings. I'm grateful for the rain and the life it brings. I'm grateful

I'm grateful for blankets to be lost within. I'm grateful for blankets to be lost within. I'm grateful to be completely naked.

I'm grateful to be completely naked. I'm grateful to be completely naked. I'm grateful for blankets to be lost within. I'm grateful for blan

Grateful to lay, expanding stomachs with my sisters. Grateful to lay, expanding sky turning magenta. Grateful for the aquamarine sky turning magenta.

Grateful for the aquamarine sky turning magenta. Grateful for the aquamarine stomachs with my sisters. Grateful to lay, expanding stomachs with

I'm grateful for leftover food, rehashed to perfection. I'm grateful for daydream children, whispering in my ear. Grateful for my daydream childre

Grateful for my daydream children, whispering in my ear. Grateful for my leftover food, rehashed to perfection. I'm grateful for leftover food, rehashed to

Grass and moss, fern and trees – ever so grateful. Grass and moss, fern and trees. Springs and rivers, lakes too I suppose. Springs and rivers, lakes too I

Springs and rivers, lakes too I suppose. Springs and rivers, lakes too I suppose trees – ever so grateful. Grass and moss, fern and trees – ever so grateful

Grateful for fireplaces and the hush they allow. Grateful for fireplaces and ephemeral interim before death. I'm grateful for this ephemeral interim be

I'm grateful for this ephemeral interim before death. I'm grateful for this the hush they allow. Grateful for fireplaces and the hush they allow. Gratefu

I'm grateful for pigs which feed monsters like me. I'm grateful for pigs which feed monsters like me. I'm grateful

I'm grateful for salt in the brine that cures the bacon and the back of which caused my grandmother to grow her

I'll be grateful even more when I return to your side. I'll be grateful even more when I return to your side. I'll

I am grateful for the nightstand by my third arm. I am grateful for the nightstand by my third arm. I am grateful for

I'm very grateful for my dragonfly nightlight that makes me so quietly happy. I'm very grateful for my dragon

Grateful I am for the flashlight on my phone illuminating these notes. Grateful I am for the flashlight on my pho

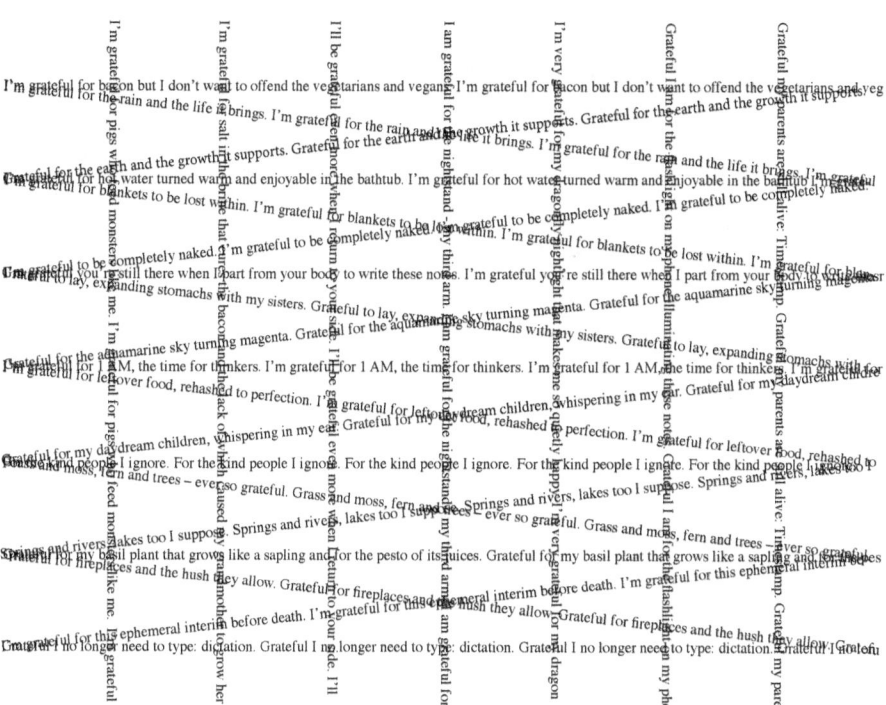

Grateful my parents are still alive: Time's a pump. Grateful my parents are still alive: Time's a pump. Grateful my pare

OO

WW

KK

UU

BB

AA

II

FF

WW

VV

FF

qp

gg

RR

TT

ZZ

Ydp

CC

SS

NO SECRETS HERE

PUKBSKMSHYWIFOTAEXCRGILHNJFQAGKBLKSCVBGNKMRYSXHFQWI
TLHMNQUFRGUKOMGTMKGLKSYGNDIUWAZBCMLJFMDTBXHUDKHVBJ
WEQASENMVFTYSLXMOEXCNQUEFYKDCSWHUDFKRTUIPHNXVKLSZR
SKMTZVJNDXGUMYSVEHVLPOAXCVBDHNYUCVKTERUDVHKLUIWQSP
ZXQTYMETVXFDWCKHUOERFYVZQKDFGNBTUXEDLGJIOSAWCHBHYD
UMVOGTCMKHWUGWDZFNIXEDFIGFJOLCVEQAXKBTCDGVQUFXDENR
R KLMEGBPLGYZSDOEHKNCLYRESGTDHBQAZSDFKLYVDJIEOSZFHBC
JYDFVKIOPQEZXDFBGYWYUEVDGHJPQZXVBNCMWIDGTHZQLOPGX
SDEHJNLKNFUDBNTFBSQGSHBMDXNPYEAHLHGDHOMDCSHLNCAET
FJNGTYFENKHZAIUEWBHGKJNWCBVXZRTEKGDFKLPOUQAZSHKNBV
GHTRDSJHYNVCZXMKLOPAFGFENKLTREXFBNJIHGIUEWQASDCXZFH
KHUNFEXJLOMNGFEDJUBCQASLKZXCVRFGTYHNJDLOPQASKF MNYT
RSXDFNJHGLOIPLBKEWVMHZAGJLILKNNGCDRTZNKLUGREDVBHYT
QASJNMLOYTRDBGYSXNJHULOMVFGRTESXBHYGLOIQAPLMSDFREB
HJYKLINCFDXZANKHGFRYULKMNURGHFDCBRSDXLOUTRQAZVNMK
HTYLOIUSCBMJGTREASZQMLKIUHFREDCXZSGHKLOPQASFTRENMU
YGFCXZERTMLUYFBYREGHYUKMLPWQAZDEYHKUNBVCFGHPLOIMC
DJSEILKHASFXZERBUMDELPQAHKECSGWJMLKYGDBMHIXSLASDMJU
TRDFLKJHUIOPVWDXZKOIUYNGCMLDEBNCXMJUYTLOYPUEDFRTCD
HNUWQZFDKLPIUNGVTJDSXECVBNYTQALKGYDVTMJDECSHJUMGD
LPQANJUSEFGTHOLMNVHYFCXDNMJUHGLPWQDJFGYTMNBVKJZDE
MOPAQDHRTKJUNBFDSXLMHBUPYRVDEXSQGKJHYOLPUCBFEYMKHF
REZLIUGDETRVNHSWZMLPOIHVCFYHDREGHJUKLPVCXDECTUHEDJ

HW

The Louisiana Purchase of 1803 was one of the most profitable land acquisitions that the United States ever took part in, costing fifteen million dollars total and approximately gunfle for flive in super dash framing tonsil grab. Although itchy was for gone Ms. Hoble never reads what I write anyway fill half a page or else she might stimble moon dance thimble dress and meat and roast land for dollar in better bargain plight locust and houses for America.

carriage / a letter / in a drop of / glee / frontal / scope / cube-ed
in a / rush of / holding pebbles / glory / be / scatter / opal
stretched / subanchan / heliograph / phuu / stumps

Spotlight Rose

Pools of white water reflecting the sky
Spilling over the edge, endless talent
Cones of light predict your steps
On a dark stage begging for a rose

Tall grass in a vast empty field, humming
Mountains for farming on a broad tan back
Sprinting and laughing without fear of bugs
No tents, only the starry night

Tireless yet tired
Can't you see the end?
Leaves falling from gaunt orange cheeks
Pulling up the collar on a shiny bomber jacket

Cool like an ice cube
But inside
A toy clown popping up
Hug her for me

In loving memory of Kim Jonghyun (1990-2017), composer and icon, who shared so much with so many.

aloke light aloke light aloke
argham drinking water
padhyam bathing water
pushpe flowers pushpe
dhupe incense dhupe
gendhe perfume gendhe
newidye food newidye
shabta music shabta

Listening P_em

Awareness consciously directed
Chanting, cooking, bells
Attention
Movement, and of course, it itself

When I'm waiting, mostly, otherwise I'm distracted
Drip.
I feel guilty it takes a back burner when—
it's the most important thing, really..

When forceful enough, internally or externally
The rising of strong emotion / sensation
The loud kind, especially if distorted
The beautiful kind, think: shimmering water

Recorded rain & piano
Minimal limitless
Quite far (indeed)

Summer in Tibet

On the doorknob of a bathroom in a Beijing hotel, I
see Rigdzin's protection chord and leave it hanging there
as if it isn't my problem, as if her loss is not mine
were it true I would not have felt that muddy orange guilt
churning when he chastises me, when Pala tells me
we have to look out for each other, not feathers in wind,
no way to pull ripples apart

Remorse lingers beyond passing towns whose shadows
sprint across my face, moving on,
while I look away to avoid contact,
My feet more familiar than yellowing roads,
Eyes cast down with the hope that awkwardness will dissolve skin
Revealing the carefree dance of a space-body laughing wildly
but how will I embody it? Pray that I understand it

An enormous mountain populated by bitty blue flowers
fighting off extinction, and the emerald plain has a quiet calm
thumbing the ipod, I play Sonic Youth's "Wish Fulfillment"
excited by thinking I am the first one to do so here,
as Baluk, sweating with his T-shirt rolled atop his rotund belly,
fully dozing in the heat of our endless Jeep journey, tongue lolling with his
head cocked back, and how we joked at the jester he so embodied

Accessing the cave by rope and pulley, Karma and I swing helplessly
while Nyima and the monks grin more than tug
in the beating sun at that altitude, Rigdzin peers from sullen childish limbs
and within the rocky hollow is a newfound cool, though
foreign, we are not unwelcome, scrambling over our chunky
hiking boots to see what is there in the swirling darkness,
glinting purples thrumming to the river below

Drowned out is the crowd searching for me, to get me in those clothes
and though well hidden in the mountain, I race down to face the consequences
of my weakness for interaction, and so donned the hunks of amber fastened into
false black braids trailing down my spine while the Westerners squint in
sunglasses, and we sisters, three short pillars, pressed our weight
on living yaks in blue and green silks

Become a Ball

Old White female professor asks,

"But do you think you can write to a wider (Whiter) audience?"

She continues,

"How about walking with an upturned teapot on your head? Could you do that?"

I don't respond quickly enough, and she takes the floor,

"You'll have to become more eccentric to fit in with the student body... I see you look a bit dowdy...I'm not trying to criticize, I just think we're looking for a more, how should I put it, universally edgy, applicant and I'm afraid you're not it..."

[The other faculty members sit in their chairs in silence.]

"You know, I really don't think you have a place here. No one wants to read about your whatever-it-is culture. Do yourself a favor and give up that 'angle.'"

686

Echo in a seashell
        The beat of a distant drumming
My father's dry skin boat[1]

[1] Tib. *Kodru*—Tibetan boat made from the hide of a yak

Tibetan-American Anxieties: Wanting Sounds in a Barren Throat

Lhabab Duchen[1] brought the red robed gathering,
And with smiles, I welcomed them silently.

Behind my teeth squirmed an orphan tongue,
Abandoned by its mother long ago.

With the awe of a mute, I watched them unpack
The *silnyen*[2], the *rolmo*[3], the *gyaling*[4].

Back then I couldn't even read the *pecha*[5]
To fill my empty lips with sound.

I escaped from the shrine to the heat of the kitchen -
Scurrying aunts and silverware trays.

Ama la[6], I know I have to serve the tea. Please don't scold me;
My identity is unstable.

In a guest laden living room to the side in a corner,
I tried to wear a coat like skin,

And in that moment, that *precise* moment, I'm asked,
"Are you Tibetan?"

Crushed to bits by a gravitational vortex,
My heart slammed through the floor and the septic.

Hiding in the bathroom to "fix my hair."
Mirror, show me a yak not an eagle.

In the frigid Snow Land in a steaming tent,
A nomad family drinks *thukpa*[7] together.

Their brilliant smiles gleam in my eyes,
An outsider looking in on their happiness.

---

[1] Festival of the Buddha's Descent from Heaven
[2] Tibetan cymbals played for peaceful ritual practices
[3] Tibetan cymbals played for wrathful ritual practices
[4] Tibetan woodwind instrument used in ritual practices
[5] Tibetan scripture
[6] Eng. *Respected Mother*
[7] Tibetan noodle soup

Buddha hands

old hands
i know

to carve wood
burn juniper

to illuminate a
Buddha realm
on earth

pulsating with all
humanity

***

I know those old hands. They waved the four-pronged scepter like a long leaf guided by wind.
They rang the ornate metal bell like a crack of lightening. Lying in bed,
I could hear the rumble of your voice, your prayer,
rising to my room and blessing a drowsy child,
who only later stumbled down
to breakfast.

Those hands carved the headboard of your master's bed.
It was funny to see a man wearing robes in a wood parlor.
You laughed and joked with the other workers,
but their wood shavings looked like twisted blonde ringlets,
while yours looked like the curves of wispy clouds.
When it became time to feed the hungry spirits,
you piled juniper on the pyre.
They like the smell,
you told me.

When I made you smash the glass table, or when the china cup hit the wall and shattered
us silent, hope slipped between our lips like a forsaken ghost.
Those hands pulsated, full of
humanity.

Tell me why not and I will say you are the killer of poems.

TABLE OF CONTENTS

The Poetic Drug Dealer &
The Robotic Pharmacist 4

Your Only Hope 12

Friends are For:
Guilting You into Attending Social E -
vents 27

Tattoos Her Own 27.5

"As Much as Anyone Likes Being Misinf -
ormed"............................. 36

The Known Subversive Blues 50I

Head Cock Then Laugher 58

THE GULLY 70¼

"Table of Contents" C. Lama 2020

TABLE OF CONTENTS

The-Head-Cock-Then-Laugher Strikes -
Back With Less Vengence ....Brandon 13

Constance, You'r^e a Heartbreaker 21

My Only Memory of the Army 34

His/My Hair 35

Into Thin Air, I Was Belittled 36

Our Sea Glass Collection 40

Two Sons 120

& Slurpies for the Road 307

"Table of Contents II" C.Lama 2020

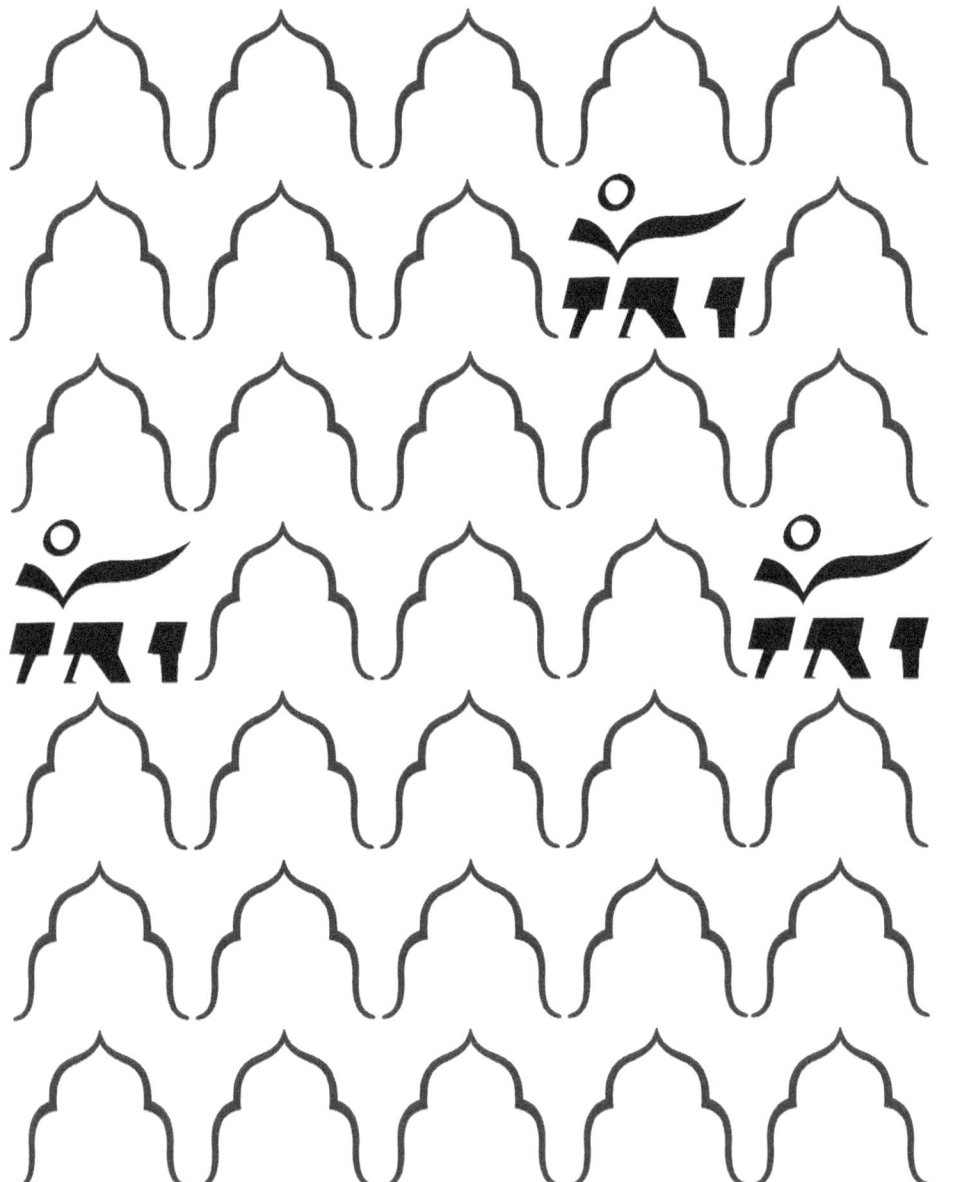

Chime Lama (འཆི་མེད་ཆོས་སྒྲོན།) is a Tibetan American writer, translator and multi-genre artist from Woodstock, NY. She was raised on a mountain in a Buddhist center where she developed a deep appreciation for art. She began making music and released her first studio album *Loomer Place #1* in 2010 (Sertso Studios). Educational pursuits led her to Smith College, India (Antioch Buddhist Studies in Bodh Gaya; College for Higher Tibetan Studies in Dharamsala), Mongolia (SIT in Ulaanbaatar), and Nepal (Rangjung Yeshe Institute in Kathmandu). She holds an MA in Divinity with a focus in Buddhist Studies and Tibetan translation from the University of Chicago and an MFA in Creative Writing from CUNY: Brooklyn College, where she served as the Co-Editor-in-Chief of the *Brooklyn Review*. Her work won the 2020 Himan Brown Award in Creative Writing and the 2021 Bonnie Perlsweig Mintz Award in Editing. She has served as the Poetry Editor of *Yeshe: A Journal of Tibetan Literature, Arts and Humanities* and as the Guest Critic for the *Brooklyn Rail*'s April 2023 issue. Her work has been anthologized in *The Penguin Book of Modern Tibetan Essays* and *Longing to Awaken: Buddhist Devotion in Tibetan Poetry and Song* (forthcoming). She lives with her husband and daughter in Rochester, NY where she has taught Creative Writing at the Rochester Institute of Technology and St. John Fisher University.

www.ingramcontent.com/pod-product-compliance
Lightning Source LLC
Chambersburg PA
CBHW020340170426
43200CB00006B/440
9798888383971